MY JOURNEY

MAINE

MINNESOTA

MICHIGAN

WISCONSIN

VT

NH

NEW YORK

MASS

CONN

RI

IOWA

MICHIGAN

Crown Point, Indiana

PENNSYLVANIA

NJ

**Purdue University
West Lafayette, Indiana**

OHIO

MD

DE

**Wright-Patterson Air Force Base
Dayton, Ohio**

ILLINOIS

INDIANA

WEST VIRGINIA

VIRGINIA

MISSOURI

KENTUCKY

NORTH CAROLINA

ARKANSAS

TENNESSEE

SOUTH CAROLINA

ATLANTIC OCEAN

MISSISSIPPI

GEORGIA

ALABAMA

LOUISIANA

**Johnson Space Center
Houston, Texas**

**Kennedy Space Center
Merritt Island, Florida**

FLORIDA

N

W E

S

GULF OF MEXICO

NORTHCREST

FORT WAYNE COMMUNITY SCHOOLS
Fort Wayne, Indiana

FWCS

WE ARE YOUR SCHOOLS

BECOMING A SPACEWALKER

BECOMING A

MY JOURNEY TO THE STARS

BY ASTRONAUT JERRY L. ROSS
WITH SUSAN G. GUNDERSON

PURDUE UNIVERSITY PRESS • WEST LAFAYETTE, INDIANA

Printed in the United States of America.

ISBN: 978-1-55753-693-8. Also available as an e-book.

Cataloging-in-Publication data on file at the Library of Congress.

PHOTO CREDITS The images in this book are used with permission and through the courtesy of: **NASA** p. 11TL, 11TR, 11M, 11B, 12T, 12B, 22B, 23B, 24T, 24B, 25, 26TL, 26B, 27T, 27B, 28TL, 28TR, 28B, 29M, 30T, 30B, 31T, 33, 34, timeline (tl.) T3-T7, T9-T11, B1-B11, cover images; **Emily Whitehouse** p. 14T, 14BL, 14BR; **U.S. Post Office** (Bureau of Engraving and Printing, designed by Charles R. Chickering) p. 18T; **Purdue Reamer Club** p. 19B; **Stephen Martin Photography** p. 32; **Library of Congress** tl. T1; **U.S. Air Force** tl. T2; **U.S. National Archives and Records Administration** tl. T8. Special thanks to Kevin Metrocavage for his help with image retrieval.

Front cover design by Mary Jane Gavenda. Back cover and book design by Heidi Branham.

This book was developed in partnership with the Purdue University College of Education, with generous support from alumni, faculty, and staff. Educational resources and digitized archive materials available at www.jerrylross.com.

CONTENTS

★ MY DREAM

As I ran across my backyard, I could see my best friend Jim already waiting for me at the edge of Grandpa's field. After supper, on many summer evenings, we met there to stargaze.

We climbed onto the stacks of freshly baled hay, positioned ourselves for comfortable viewing, and waited for the show to begin. The sky turned from blue to black. The shimmering stars, the planets, and the galaxies slowly revealed themselves. It was such an awe-inspiring display that we often lay quietly, lost in our own thoughts.

One night, I broke the silence. "You know what, Jim? Someday people are going to go up in space."

Jim wasn't so sure. "Yeah, right," he chuckled.

"No, I'm serious," I said. "One day people are going to go up there. And I'm going to be one of them."

Jim wasn't so sure because the year was 1957. At that point in history, no human being had ever been launched into outer space.

But change was coming. Scientists and engineers were making new discoveries about spaceflight. And I was curious. I wanted to know what was out there in the stars.

So I became a kid with a seemingly impossible dream for the time. I wanted to journey into space.

How did I become a record-setting, spacewalking astronaut?

Read my story to find out . . .

SCHOOL DAYS 1956 –1957
Washington Elementary
Jerry L. Ross

☆ THE BEGINNING

I grew up in the country near the northwest Indiana town of Crown Point. Can you locate Crown Point on the map inside the front cover?

My mom, dad, sisters Judi and Janet, and I lived in this white frame house. It was built by my dad and my uncles. There were two bedrooms, a kitchen, a dining room, a living room, and one bathroom.

For a while, Judi and I shared an upstairs bedroom. Then when I was five years old, Janet was born, and Dad built a bedroom for me next to the new oil furnace in the basement. My room was cool in the summer and toasty warm in the winter. Over the years, I got a lot of thinking, dreaming, and planning done in my private corner of the house.

My basement bedroom window is on the right. Can you find it?

Mom

Phyllis Elaine Ross,
my mom

Mom ran our house. She was the grocery shopper, cook, cleaner, reader of books, and maker of house rules. She would say: "Don't bang the door!" "Stop teasing your sisters!" "Did you finish your homework?" Education was very important to her.

Mom always encouraged my sisters and me to learn and to try new things that might be considered beyond our reach.

Dad

Donald John Ross,
my dad

Dad worked nearly his whole life at the U.S. Steel Mill in Gary, Indiana. He worked in the blast furnace maintenance division. Sometimes he worked seven days a week for twelve hours a day.

But Dad still found time to coach my Little League baseball teams and hit fly balls to my friend Jim and me. Jim was a Chicago White Sox fan, but he still rode along with Dad and me to Wrigley Field in Chicago to watch Dad's and my favorite baseball team—the Cubs.

Dad never gave up on the Cubs winning the World Series. "Next year will be *the* year!" he'd optimistically say.

Grandparents

My Grandpa and Grandma Joe Ross were my dad's parents. Grandpa Joe was a farmer, and he and Grandma were our neighbors. From our yard, I could look across the cornfields and see their house and barns.

One day, when I was four years old, I was playing in our backyard when I thought: *I wonder what Grandpa Joe and Grandma Joe are doing? I'll just hike on over for a quick visit and maybe a cookie or two.* The corn was almost as tall as the top of my head. With my dog Prancer leading the way, we navigated toward their house, zigzagging through the rows of corn.

Grandpa Joe and me with my dog, Prancer.

Mom noticed I was missing from our yard. In a panic, she called Grandma Joe on the phone. "Jerry's missing. Have you seen him?"

"Hang on . . . let me check." Grandma looked out their back window. "Here he comes. I can see his head bobbing along just above the corn."

I made a few exploratory trips across that field. Grandpa Joe would bring me home. Mom would thank him and sigh, "This kid is just too curious."

My Grandma and Grandpa Dillabaugh were my mom's parents. They lived over on the main highway a mile from my house. Grandma baked delicious desserts. Grandpa ran a house moving business.

Walking into Grandpa Dillabaugh's workshop was like stepping into another world. Everywhere I looked there were tools and equipment for digging, sawing, hammering, and drilling. The shelves were crammed with paint cans, boxes of nails, and jars of screws. Giant loops of chains hung on one wall.

Grandpa and I took things apart. We hunted for old electric motors in the town junkyard and hauled them back to his shop. I pulled a wooden box over to his workbench and stepped up to watch. Grandpa showed me how to unscrew the back of a motor and extract the copper wire. I asked questions: "Why'd you use that screwdriver, Grandpa?" "How does that motor use electricity?" "Can I try to lift that sledgehammer?"

I watched and I learned. I noticed that every job required a certain kind of tool, and every tool had a specific purpose. Being able to select the right tool made the work go faster.

This picture was taken of Grandpa Dillabaugh and me outside his workshop.

When I got older, my job was to be Grandpa's assistant. Once, when I was helping him fix a broken well motor, I got confused about which way to turn the screwdriver to tighten a screw. Grandpa said, "Remember this: righty-tighty, lefty-loosey."

I never forgot.

KID STUFF

When I was growing up in the 1950s, my sisters, friends, and I entertained ourselves by inventing our own fun. For example, there were no public swimming pools in Crown Point. So on blistering hot northern Indiana summer days, my sister Judi and I cooled off in our own pool.

First, we pulled on our swimsuits. Next, we dragged the old metal washtub into the backyard. Then, we filled the tub with chilly water from the hose and plopped in. We just fit!

Remember this very important fact for later in my story: I never learned how to swim. I tried and tried in nearby Lake Michigan. But I sank in the water like a rock tossed into a pond. Every time.

Just off the back steps of my house was a dirt pile that was perfect for practicing plowing with my toy tractor. Do you see those trees in the distance? Keep reading to find out what I lost in those trees.

I loved the sensation of swinging. I pumped my legs to propel the swing higher and higher. Then I would leap out. Just for a second, it felt like I was flying. But gravity pulled me back down to Earth. **THUD.**

My best friend Jim and I were rugged explorers. We hiked the fields and investigated the ponds, marshes, and creeks. We tracked wild animals, built dams, and watched the sky.

At the back corner of our yard Jim and I built roads. First, we dug a pit. Then, we used bottles to transport water to the pit where we mixed water and sand. Old boards worked to grade and smooth our roads.

Jim and I were proud of our brand new bikes. That summer we pedaled all over the countryside in search of adventures. My little sister Janet was more impressed with her suitcase.

☆ THE SPACE AGE

In the fall of 1957, I began the 4th grade while American scientists and engineers were successfully launching rockets toward outer space. Scientists even predicted that humans might one day venture out into the stars and live on orbiting space stations. This really captured my imagination.

WASHINGTON GRADE 4 1957 - 1958

My teacher was Mrs. Effie Laney. She was the kind of teacher who made her students want to learn. She encouraged and inspired us. She made learning fun.

For me, Friday, October 4, 1957, was a normal school day. At lunch I traded my cookies for a candy bar. We played marbles at recess and I won.

I got an "A" on my arithmetic test. But when I clicked off my bedroom light that night, little did I know that on Saturday I would wake up to shocking news. Television and radio bulletins announced to alarmed Americans that the Soviet Union had launched the first man-made orbiting satellite, *Sputnik 1*. The newsman said, "The world will never be the same. This is the start of the Space Age."

On Monday morning, Mrs. Laney, my teacher, told us that *Sputnik* was the first object humans had launched into space that did not fall back to Earth. It stayed in orbit. This excited me beyond words.

I read that *Sputnik* might be visible in the evening sky shortly after sunset. So for many nights, I stood in our front yard scanning the heavens. I wanted so badly to see *Sputnik* scooting across the night sky.

But, I never did.

Making a Scrapbook

I wanted to learn even more about satellites and rockets. For a while, I'd been searching for pictures and articles in newspapers and magazines that my aunts and uncles saved for me. I cut out the articles and studied them. After the launch of *Sputnik* and America's first man-made satellite, *Explorer 1*, newspapers and magazines exploded with space news.

One afternoon, Mom watched me sort through my pile of articles.

"What if I help you organize your collection?" Mom asked. "We could paste them into a scrapbook. You can add to the blank pages as you find more."

The next day, when I got home from school, Mom presented me with a brand new scrapbook.

"Gee, thanks, Mom! But how do I start?"

Mom helped me. We sat down at the kitchen table. We reread all the articles and sorted the pictures. Mom asked me questions about the graphs and diagrams. We discussed facts. Talking about the facts helped me write captions. Mom typed the captions, and I pasted them under the pictures.

When we were finished, I had the beginning of my own book of current news about rockets, satellites, and space travel. I was learning how to find answers to my questions. And, I was discovering what was going to happen next in America's space program.

All through grade school I collected space news. Eventually, I filled four scrapbooks with articles, pictures, and captions. Turn the page to see two pages from a scrapbook Mom helped me make.

Sputnik 1 was launched by the Soviet Union on October 4, 1957. It is the world's first man-made satellite. It started the Space Race between the Soviets and the United States.

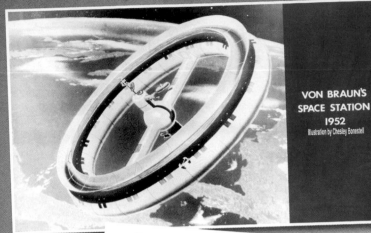

VON BRAUN'S
SPACE STATION
1952
Illustration by Chesley Bonestell

A space station in
the future.

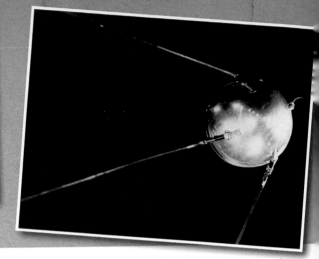

Sputnik 1 was launched by the Soviet
Union on October 4, 1957. It is the
world's first man-made satellite. It
started the Space Race between the
Soviets and the United States.

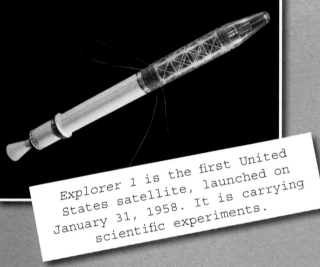

Explorer 1 is the first United
States satellite, launched on
January 31, 1958. It is carrying
scientific experiments.

WHAT MAKES A GOOD SPACEMAN?

A spaceman cannot be just anybody. In spaceflight, a person must take care of himself and his spaceship. He has to be "wide awake" to watch and keep records.

Captain Kincheloe is a good spaceman. He finished college at Purdue University, but he is still learning new things. He is interested in flying, space, and science.

A GOOD SPACEMAN MUST ALSO BE:
√ *healthy and strong*. A strong body and a healthy mind are needed to pass the test of space flying.
√ *brave*. Courage is needed to explore the unknown areas in space.
√ *calm*. He does not get upset easily. He must have a steady hand and must think clearly.
√ *able to live in a tiny cabin*. Every inch of space aboard a spaceship is used carefully.

A GOOD SPACEMAN IS NOT AFRAID OF:
√ *heights or of being alone*. He may have to spend long periods of time by himself. . .high above the earth.
√ *work*. He has several jobs to do in space.

Captain Iven Kincheloe is the first
spaceman. He is the first pilot to
fly above 100,000 feet. He flew the
X-2, a rocket-powered plane, at
more than 2,000 miles per hour.

WEEKLY READER March 1958

The first American astronauts are called the Mercury 7. They are all test pilots.
First row (left to right): Wally Schirra, Deke Slayton, John Glenn, Scott Carpenter.
Second row (left to right): Alan Shepard, Gus Grissom, Gordon Cooper.

This is the X-15 rocket-powered space plane. The pilot's name is Neil Armstrong. He went to college at Purdue University. He is a test pilot at Edwards Air Force Base in California.

A PLAN

The more I added to my scrapbook, the more I learned. For instance, I discovered that the people doing space work had gone to college. Some were scientists or engineers. Some were pilots.

I learned that engineers used arithmetic to figure out how many rocket stages were needed to launch a payload into outer space. I thought: *I'm good at arithmetic. I love science. I could do that.*

Then I read that many of the engineers graduated from Purdue University. I thought: *Purdue is in Indiana! Maybe I could go to Purdue? Maybe I could even become an engineer?* Right then, at ten years old, I set my sights on going to Purdue. I made it my goal.

But I needed a plan. First, I figured that I would need good grades to be admitted to Purdue. I thought: *I don't get straight A's, but I study hard. I can get the grades.*

Second, I would need money to pay for classes, food, and a place to live. The cost was a problem. I concluded that my parents might not be able to afford to send me *and* my sisters to college.

Then I thought: *I have a few years. Maybe I could save enough money to help my parents?*

I spilled out the coins in my money jar. I counted four dollars and sixty-seven cents. It was a start. But if I was going to save enough, I was going to have to get a job.

But who would give a job to a ten-year-old kid?

Kid for Hire

Mom and Dad spread the word that I was looking for work so I could save money for college. I didn't get paid much. For a dollar an hour I painted fences, baled hay, trimmed pine trees, and mowed yards.

A neighboring farmer hired Jim and me to help vaccinate 400 chickens. We worked at night because the sleepy roosting hens were easier to sneak up on. The farmer showed us how to grab a hen by the legs and flip her upside down. Then we were instructed to carry the hen to the farmer. He administered the vaccination.

The hens were not at all happy about the whole thing. For two hours, in the dark, we hustled back and forth from the henhouse to the farmer carrying squawking chickens.

Around midnight, Jim pointed out a few hens roosting in a tree in the chicken yard. Before Jim could stop me, I shinnied up the tree. Balancing my feet on a branch, I reached up and grabbed four hens by their legs—two in *each* hand. The hens whipped their wings in my face. My feet slipped. I tightened my grip and jumped to keep from falling. All four chickens flapped their wings wildly.

Meanwhile, Jim was watching this whole scene unfold from below. By the time I hit the ground, still holding onto the four hens, Jim was rolling around in the dirt, laughing so hard he could hardly breathe. Between gasps he said that it looked like I was trying to use the chickens to fly.

Saving

After a few weeks of work, my money jar was overflowing. Mom drove me to the First National Bank of Crown Point where I opened a savings account. Every time I deposited money, the bank teller added it to my balance.

It made me feel good to see my money grow. It made me want to work even harder.

Here is the second page of my bank book. Can you find the largest deposit? Can you find my only withdrawal?

I saved for college, for model rockets, and later for a small motorcycle to drive myself to jobs.

WITHDRAWAL	DEPOSIT	DATE	INTEREST	BALANCE
		JUN 30	2.25	187.78 CP 1
	2.25	JUL 11		190.03 CP 1
		DEC 30	2.25	192.28 CP 1
	10.00	JAN 29		202.28 CP 1
	5.00	JUN 2		207.28 CP 1
		JUN 30	3.00	210.28 CP 1
50.00		OCT 25		160.28 CP 1
		DEC 31	2.40	162.68 CP 1
	7.00	JAN 31		169.68 CP 1
	21.00	MAR 9		190.68 CP 1
	28.00	MAY 9		218.68 CP 1
	100.00	JUN 11		318.68 CP 1
	27.00	JUN 24		345.68 CP 2 A
		JUN 29	2.80	348.48 CP 2 A
	31.00	JUL 12		379.48 CP 2 A
	26.00	AUG 15		405.48 CP 1 B
	57.00	SEP 5		462.48 CP 2 B
	8.00	SEP 12		470.48 CP 2 B
	14.00	SEP 21		484.48 CP 2 B
	10.00	SEP 26		494.48 CP 2 A
		DEC 31	6.65	501.13 CP 2 A
	5.00	MAR 3		506.13 CP 2 A
	29.00	MAY 28		535.13 CP 1 B
	24.00	JUN 9		559.13 CP 1 B
		JUN 30	7.65	566.78 CP 1 B
	37.57	JUL 21		604.35 CP 1 B

THE FIRST NATIONAL BANK OF CROWN POINT

OLDEST BANK IN LAKE COUNTY

SCIENTIFIC CURIOSITY

I wanted to learn how rockets were propelled into the sky. So I began buying and experimenting with model rockets. I constructed a backyard launch pad, a place to blast my rockets into the sky. I took detailed notes about every rocket's engine size, its payload, launch conditions, how high it flew, and where it was found in the surrounding fields when it fell back to Earth.

Remember the trees off in the distance from my house? I lost several rockets that got caught in the top branches of those trees.

One afternoon, I was considering what I should launch as a payload in my biggest rocket. Suddenly, I was overcome by a wave of scientific curiosity so intense that it could not be ignored. *Ah-ha! My little sister Janet has a pet white mouse.*

I found Janet reading on the couch. "Hey, Janet, wouldn't it be neat if your mouse could be the first Indiana mouse to be launched in a rocket?"

Her face clouded over. "**NO!** It would **NOT!**"

"He will be fine. Really. You watched me launch crickets. They hopped away."

She began to soften, so I took advantage of the moment.

I carefully loaded the mouse into the payload compartment at the top of the rocket. We began the countdown: ". . . 5 . . . 4 . . . 3 . . . 2 . . . 1 . . . zero!" I pushed the ignition button. *WHOOSH!* The rocket shot skyward. But, it suddenly spiraled off to the right. We watched in horror as it spun up and over, corkscrewed down nose first, and drilled straight into the hard earth.

Later, I pored over my notes trying to figure out what went wrong. In the end, I learned that just one small miscalculation could impact the success or failure of a rocket launch—and sadly, the life of our little space explorer.

Junior High Revelations

During the summer before 7ᵗʰ grade, my family and I visited the Museum of Science and Industry in Chicago, Illinois. My sisters and I loved the interactive exhibits. Visitors were actually encouraged to push buttons and pull levers. This place was like heaven for a curious kid like me!

On that trip, Dad surprised us by stopping at Midway Airport. He bought tickets on a six-seat propeller plane for the whole family to take a flight-seeing tour of downtown Chicago. It was my very first time flying!

We swooped around the city skyscrapers. My forehead pressed against the window, I looked down at the square city blocks, boats on Lake Michigan, and the winding Chicago River. I was seeing a bird's-eye view of Earth. I twisted my head to peer up at the clouds. I wondered what it would look like from even higher up.

During the summer before 8ᵗʰ grade, I decided that I wanted to play on the basketball team. So all summer I practiced shooting layups and free throws. When school started in the fall, I tried out and made the team. I played in some games. Under the basket, I got bonked by other players' elbows on the top of my head.

Can you find me in this picture of the Crown Point 8ᵗʰ grade basketball team? Why do you think playing high school basketball was not in my future?

High School Choices

By the time I started high school in the fall of 1962, America had successfully launched astronauts into space. We were locked in a race with the Russians to land the first man on the moon. I was even more determined to get into the engineering program at Purdue University.

In high school, I took the math, science, and English courses required for entry into the engineering program. I worked all sorts of jobs, still saving for my college fund. I studied hard. My grades were good. I hoped they were good enough. During my senior year, I mailed my application to Purdue.

Then, one day, I came home from school to find an official letter from the Purdue University Office of Admissions waiting for me. I thought: *Well, this is it*. I tore open the envelope and unfolded the letter. I was accepted! I was going to Purdue!

But I found out that at Purdue I would have to choose between military officer training and physical education swimming classes. Swimming would be a problem because I still couldn't swim. I still sank like a rock every time I was in the water.

So I chose Air Force officer training classes because I knew that the Air Force was doing most of the military space work. This choice would take me on a path to be trained as an engineer and an Air Force pilot, and maybe even to become an astronaut—and fly in space!

Jerry L. Ross, 1966
Crown Point High School

The night before I left for Purdue's campus in West Lafayette, I packed my stuff. Sitting on the edge of my bed, I thought about all the planning and dreaming I had done in my little basement room.

Then a realization hit me. I was leaving my home, my family, and the flatlands and farm fields of northern Indiana—everything I had ever known. I was going off to a completely different world. I was going on an amazing adventure!

Purdue University

My parents drove me to Purdue's campus in West Lafayette, Indiana. They helped me move into my room at Circle Pines Cooperative, a residence for 40 male students. I stood on the front steps and watched my parents drive away. I thought: *Well, here I go. Whatever happens next is up to me.* Can you find Purdue on the map?

At Circle Pines, we all worked together to clean, to buy groceries, and to cook for ourselves. We learned about planning, organizing, and leadership. We also had fun!

Fall semester meant the sights, sounds, and traditions of Big Ten football. Students decorated residences for homecoming weekend.

Football game days were electrifying. Boisterous fans packed the stadium. There was the *rat-a-tat-tat* of the marching band drums and the clanging of the Boilermaker Special's brass bell. When Purdue scored its first touchdown, the stadium erupted with a deafening roar.

We constructed a mammoth-sized mixer operated by Purdue Pete to "whip up" the Northwestern Wildcats.

This is the Boilermaker Special, the official mascot of Purdue University.

After a big game, students sometimes celebrated an exciting win by tearing down the stadium's goalposts. Do you know what my two Circle Pines buddies and I are showing off?

During the second semester, I got caught up in the fun of college life and got a "D" in calculus. **GULP.** I felt like I had swallowed a brick. I decided that I was *not* going to fail. From that point on, I worked harder and improved my grades.

Then, during my sophomore year, I was slammed with unexpected news. An Air Force eye doctor disqualified me for pilot training. In an instant, it seemed my dreams of becoming a pilot and an astronaut—and traveling into space—ended. I was utterly devastated.

So what did I do? I adjusted my plan. I thought: *I will still graduate as an engineer and an Air Force officer. So maybe I could be an Air Force engineer and work in America's space program?* It felt good to stay focused on a goal.

Later that year, I attended a student club meeting, never imagining that I would meet Karen Pearson, my future wife. When I saw Karen across the room, my heart did a flip-flop.

During our senior year, Karen and I got married. That spring, I graduated with a degree in mechanical engineering, and I was commissioned as a Second Lieutenant in the United States Air Force. I stayed enrolled at Purdue and worked as a graduate research assistant in the Jet Propulsion Laboratory. A year later, our daughter, Amy Jo Ross, was born.

My five and one-half years at Purdue were amazing. I began my freshman year as a shy country kid with a dream. Now I was a mechanical engineer with a master's degree and an officer in the United States Air Force.

It was time to move on to a new chapter of my life.

SUPERSONIC FLIGHT

My first official Air Force orders took my family and me to the Aero Propulsion Laboratory at Wright-Patterson Air Force Base near Dayton, Ohio. Can you find it on the map?

Around this same time, NASA began designing a new space vehicle called the Space Shuttle. It would transport crews and payloads into space and return to Earth to land on a runway. Most important to me, *engineers* could be selected as crewmembers. I could still become an astronaut!

This is the Air Force Test Pilot School patch I wore on my flight suit. Keep reading to see other patches representing steps on my journey.

My next Air Force orders sent me to a school where I would learn to be a flight test engineer in supersonic jets. Karen and I packed up our daughter Amy and our son Scott. We moved from the leafy green Midwest to the treeless desert of southern California. Travel west on the map to find Edwards Air Force Base.

My first flight as a student flight test engineer was in a KC-135 refueling tanker. To test the plane, the pilot flew up-and-down and side-to-side maneuvers. Strapped into the cargo bay, I felt like I was riding a roller coaster in the sky. When we finally landed, I took my queasy, wobbly, airsick self straight home to lie down. My wife Karen said she'd never seen a person that shade of pea green.

Eventually, I flew in twenty different types of aircraft. I never turned green again!

Two years after our arrival at Edwards, I applied for the first class of NASA Space Shuttle astronauts, along with 8,000 other men and women. Only 35 applicants would be selected for the first class.

As a flight test engineer, I flew on the supersonic B-1A bomber at Edwards Air Force Base from 1976 to 1979.

During the candidate selection process, I advanced through to the top group of finalists. I was so excited! Becoming a Space Shuttle astronaut was within my reach!

TRY, TRY AGAIN

I was **not** selected. For a time, I thought it might be the end of my dream. Then, good news! The Air Force sent me to NASA's Johnson Space Center, where I would work as an Air Force payload officer. Karen and I packed up our family and moved to Houston, Texas. Which direction did we travel from California?

At Johnson Space Center, other engineers and I planned how the first Space Shuttle flights would carry satellites and scientific experiments into space. I had reached my goal of becoming an engineer working in America's space program.

But I still longed to fly in space. When NASA announced another astronaut selection, I anxiously applied *again*.

Months later, my phone rang with the call I'd been waiting for. When I started leaping around, co-workers knew I had been selected for the next astronaut class. Now I wanted to qualify to be a spacewalking astronaut.

But, there was a *big* problem. To be a spacewalker, an astronaut must pass a swimming test. I still couldn't even float. So I tried more lessons. After a few frustrating attempts, the instructor said, "You're right. You can't swim."

I was worried this one problem would end my dream. But NASA allowed me to earn my SCUBA certification instead of passing a swimming test. Now I was closer to my ultimate goal of walking in space!

After I became an astronaut, other engineers and I developed the tools and procedures that could be used to build a space station, a habitable structure that would orbit the Earth. Building a space station would be a colossal undertaking because in space there are extreme temperature changes, no gravity, no air, and no handy building supply stores nearby.

This is me defying gravity with a mid-air flip on my first zero-gravity training flight. *Whoopee!*

Then, it was **finally** my turn to ride a rocket into space.

My first Space Shuttle flight began on a crystal clear night at Kennedy Space Center, November 26, 1985. Can you find Kennedy Space Center on Merritt Island, Florida, on the map?

Dressed in our flight suits, six other crewmembers and I arrived at the launch pad. I was awestruck at the sight of the Space Shuttle *Atlantis*. It was no longer just a space vehicle waiting silently on the pad. Now it was filled with tons of rocket fuel. It hissed and groaned. Clouds of super-cooled air billowed. Energy radiated. It seemed like *Atlantis* was alive.

We rode up the launch pad elevator, entered the Shuttle, and strapped into our seats. During the next three hours, we completed our prelaunch tasks.

At five minutes before launch, the Shuttle's auxiliary power units were started and our seats began to vibrate. As the countdown proceeded, everything seemed to be happening faster and faster.

At six seconds before launch, the three main engines roared to life. I felt the whole Shuttle shaking on the pad. In my head I counted down the final seconds: . . . *5 . . . 4 . . . 3 . . . 2 . . . 1 . . . zero. Ignition! Liftoff!*

In a thunderous explosion, the solid rocket boosters ignited and the Shuttle roared off the launch pad. *Atlantis* accelerated upward and rolled to the right. In 40 seconds we were moving faster than 760 miles per hour— the speed of sound. We hurtled toward space, our speed increasing. Our trajectory started to bend. We began moving more parallel to Earth's surface. Acceleration continued. Invisible G-forces pinned us back into our seats. I felt like I weighed 600 pounds.

In about eight and one-half minutes after liftoff, at just the right speed and altitude, the Shuttle's main engines shut down. *Atlantis* was in low orbit around the Earth. We unstrapped and floated in weightlessness. If I could have stood on a scale, here's what I would have weighed: zero!

This is the crew posing for a picture on the aft flight deck. Notice the popped up collars on our shirts? We weren't trying to look cool for the picture. It's just that in zero gravity everything floats . . . even our collars.

After three days spent working inside the Shuttle, at last it was time for me to go on my first spacewalk. I couldn't stop grinning as crewmembers helped me climb into my space suit. Once my tools and equipment were securely in place, we opened the airlock hatch. I floated out into inky blackness 200 miles above the Earth's surface.

I was not prepared for the vastness of space—billions and billions of stars, millions of light years away. *Infinity.*

But no time for stargazing—my spacewalking partner and I had six hours of work to do.

The rectangular-shaped device on the end of the robotic arm is a tool board— a special bench to hold spacewalkers' tools.

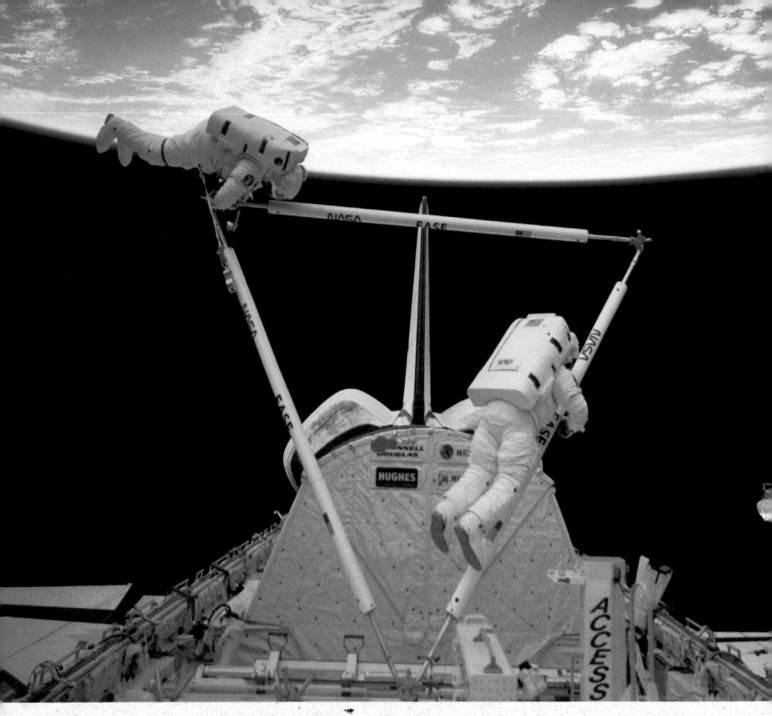

Our job was to demonstrate that parts of a structure transported from Earth in the Shuttle could be assembled in the hostile environment of space. These were the very first steps leading to the design and construction of the International Space Station. Can you find me? I have red stripes on my space suit.

While we were erecting this structure, using specialized space tools, we floated outside the Shuttle payload bay in zero gravity. We were flying around the Earth at orbit speed, or nearly five miles per *second*. Imagine that! Our speed was 17,500 miles per hour!

But since there is no air in space, there is no friction. So, the sensation of speed is different than it is on Earth. It felt as if we were drifting gently around the Earth instead of hurtling through space.

After almost seven days of working in space, it was time for us to get ready to go home. We closed the payload bay doors, stowed equipment, and strapped ourselves into our seats.

It took millions of pounds of fuel for *Atlantis* to build up enough speed to leave Earth. Now to return to Earth, the commander fired the engines to reduce our speed. Earth's gravity pulled *Atlantis* back into the atmosphere. We glided down to our landing site at Edwards Air Force Base in southern California.

First, the back wheels touched down. Next, the nose wheel hit the runway. **THUD.**

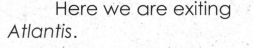

Here we are exiting *Atlantis*.

Notice how some of us are holding on to both railings and looking down. After floating around weightless for seven days, our bodies were trying to adjust to standing up. Touching the railings helped our brains remember where to put our feet.

Can you find me? I'm wearing sunglasses. At that exact moment, here's what I was thinking: *Awesome. When do I get to do this again?*

Well, I did. I flew as a mission specialist on six more Shuttle flights.

Life in Zero Gravity

Traveling on the Space Shuttle was like going on a camping trip. Once in orbit, the other crewmembers and I unpacked our stuff, set up a kitchen called the galley, and activated the toilet. Then we got to work.

But living in zero gravity changed how we ate, how we exercised, and how we slept.

For example, before a Shuttle flight, each crewmember made his or her meal choices from a special menu of Earth foods.

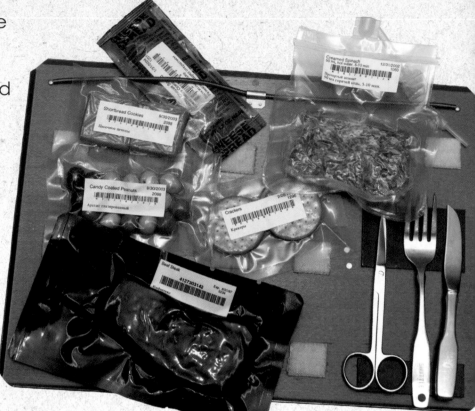

Do you recognize any of these Earth foods?

The foods were specially packaged, labeled, and loaded onto the Shuttle for space travel.

At mealtime, we velcroed our food packages to our meal trays. Magnetized silverware stuck to the tray so that equipment and crewmembers would be safe from floating forks and knives.

The toilet on the Shuttle was like a portable toilet with a vacuum cleaner attached. When a crewmember used the toilet, thigh bars kept him or her from floating off the seat. And, no room in the cramped Shuttle for a full bathroom door—just a curtain!

When people move around on Earth, the force of gravity provides resistance to keep bones and muscles strong. To stay fit in zero gravity, we exercised on special cycles, treadmills, and weight-lifting machines.

At night we zipped ourselves into sleeping bags attached to Shuttle walls, floors, and ceilings. This kept us from floating around and bumping into experiments or other snoozing crewmembers.

Every orbit the Shuttle made around Earth revealed a changing view of the continents, oceans, forests, jungles, mountains, and deserts. I wanted to see it all. So on most of my Shuttle flights, I positioned my sleeping bag next to a window. While other crewmembers were sleeping, I stayed up late watching the world go by. I didn't want to miss a single view of our spectacular Earth from 200 miles high.

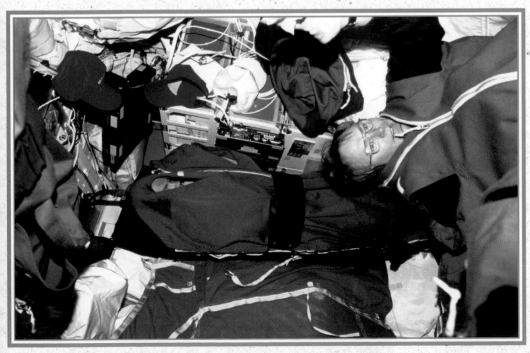

Can you find me and another crewmember zipped in for the night?

On my second Shuttle flight, we flew over Indiana. I looked down at my hometown, Crown Point. I remembered when my best friend Jim and I would lie on hay bales, gaze up at the night sky, and wonder what was out there in the stars.

28

Space Family

My family at Kennedy Space Center in Florida before my fifth Shuttle flight.
Left to right: My wife Karen, Amy, me, Scott, and my mom Phyllis Ross.

While I was involved in the space program, members of my family also were connected to space, each in a different way.

For example, my wife Karen and her Space Food Processing team purchased, cooked, freeze-dried, and packaged the foods for Shuttle and International Space Station crews.

Amy graduated from Purdue University and began her engineering career at NASA. Part of her job was to develop new versions of space gloves and certify them for astronauts to use for spacewalks. I tested Amy's gloves in space on the first International Space Station assembly flight. Today, Space Station astronauts wear the gloves Amy helped develop.

When I was home between launches, my son Scott and I rebuilt a 1957 Chevy. The car parts came to us in boxes and baskets. It was quite the puzzle. Later, I took the car key with me into space.

Do you remember the first scrapbook my mom helped me make? That scrapbook was the beginning of my journey to space.

Frequent Flyer

My last Space Shuttle flight was STS-110 in April 2002. At the exact moment *Atlantis* thundered off the pad at Kennedy Space Center in Florida, I became the first human being in history to be launched into space seven times.

It took three days of space travel for the Shuttle to catch up with the orbiting International Space Station. When it came into sight, I was reminded of my first two spacewalks. The purpose of those spacewalks was to demonstrate that astronauts could build a structure in space. I thought: *And here it is!* Today the International Space Station is the length and width of a football field. Inside are four research laboratories, two gyms, two kitchens, sleeping areas, and two bathrooms. Six crewmembers live on board and conduct experiments.

This was my last walk in space. When I reluctantly entered the airlock of the International Space Station, I knew that this chapter of my life had come to an end.

MY NEXT MISSION

So where did life take me after my last Shuttle flight?

Without leaving the ground, I stayed as closely connected to Space Shuttle launches and spaceflight as possible. I led an engineering team that provided technical support to Space Shuttle and International Space Station crews, helping them prepare for

their missions. I escorted Shuttle crews to the launch pad, and I greeted them on the runway when they returned to Earth.

This picture of the International Space Station was taken by the crew of the departing Space Shuttle *Atlantis* in July 2011. It was the final flight of the Shuttle program. A few months later, I retired.

Nowadays, I travel around the country talking with kids and adults about my experiences. Sometimes they ask me, "Of all that you have accomplished and of all the honors you have received, which are you most proud of?"

I tell them that I'm proud to have served our country by working in two challenging, exciting, and important space exploration projects—the Space Shuttle program and the International Space Station. I'm proud to have fulfilled my dream of flying in space. And, I'm proud that when the Crown Point Community School Corporation built a new elementary school, it was named *Jerry Ross Elementary School*.

★ MY CHALLENGE TO YOU

I was ten years old when I decided that I would go to Purdue University, learn to be an engineer, and work in our country's space program. Pursuing those goals became a long journey of discovery and adventure. I planned. I worked. I saved. I tried to learn everything I could about spaceflight. When an obstacle appeared in my path, I tried another way. I kept believing that I could.

You can do this, too. What are you curious about? What do you love to do? Where could this take you?

Then, make good choices. Do your best. Study hard. Work hard.

And don't give up too easily, because your dream can come true.

Jerry Ross Elementary School, Crown Point, Indiana

The "Spacewalker" in my "office," surrounded by the International Space Station and the Space Shuttle *Atlantis*. Can you find me?

At liftoff on STS-27, the Space Shuttle's three main engines and two large, white solid rocket boosters combined to generate over 6.5 million pounds of thrust. It was a great ride!

These patches represent my seven Space Shuttle missions.

Can you locate my name on each patch?